Our Lady's Beads of Love

A Story of the Rosary

Susan Glynn Mulé

Razumov Publishing

Copyright © 2025 Susan Glynn Mulé
All rights reserved.
No part of this publication may be reproduced, stored in a retrieval system, or transmitted in any form or by any means—electronic, mechanical, photocopying, recording, or otherwise—without prior written permission of the publisher, except in the case of brief quotations used in reviews or articles.
ISBN 979-8-9937218-0-4
Published by Razumov Publications, Sugar Land, Texas
For registration pending with the U.S. Copyright Office
Cover and interior illustrations were created using digital tools, including AI-assisted methods, and were further edited, arranged, and refined by the author to achieve a consistent watercolor style.
Printed in the United States of America

To the "Littles" of
Saint Laurence Catholic Church
for whom this story was written.
--Susan Glynn Mulé

Long ago, before there were cars, phones, or even big cities with skyscrapers, people still wanted to pray and talk to God.

Back then, most people could not read. Even if someone could read, books were hard to get and very expensive. There were no computers back then, nor any other way to print things. Every book had to be copied out by hand.

So people found a simple way to pray— by counting their prayers on pebbles or knots!

People knew that there were 150 Psalms in the Bible and that monks prayed them every day. So, they often tried to say 150 prayers every day. Usually, these prayers were repetitions of the Our Father or the Hail Mary.

Each pebble or knot reminded them to say an Our Father or a Hail Mary.

Every day, a kind priest named Saint

Dominic prayed very hard for peace in the world.

Saint Dominic wanted everyone
to pray for peace.
He also prayed for all of the people
to have an easier
way to keep track of their prayers.

One day, Saint Dominic was praying in the Church of Prouille in France. He asked Mary, the Mother of Jesus, for help.

"Our Lady," he pleaded, "please ask Jesus to send something to help the people pray."

As Saint Dominic prayed, something wonderful happened!

Mary, the Mother of Jesus, appeared to him, holding a special string of beads. She called it "The Rosary". She told Saint Dominic that each prayer would be like giving her a rose for Jesus.

Smiling gently, Our Lady said, "Tell everyone to pray my Rosary. Each bead will bring peace to their hearts."

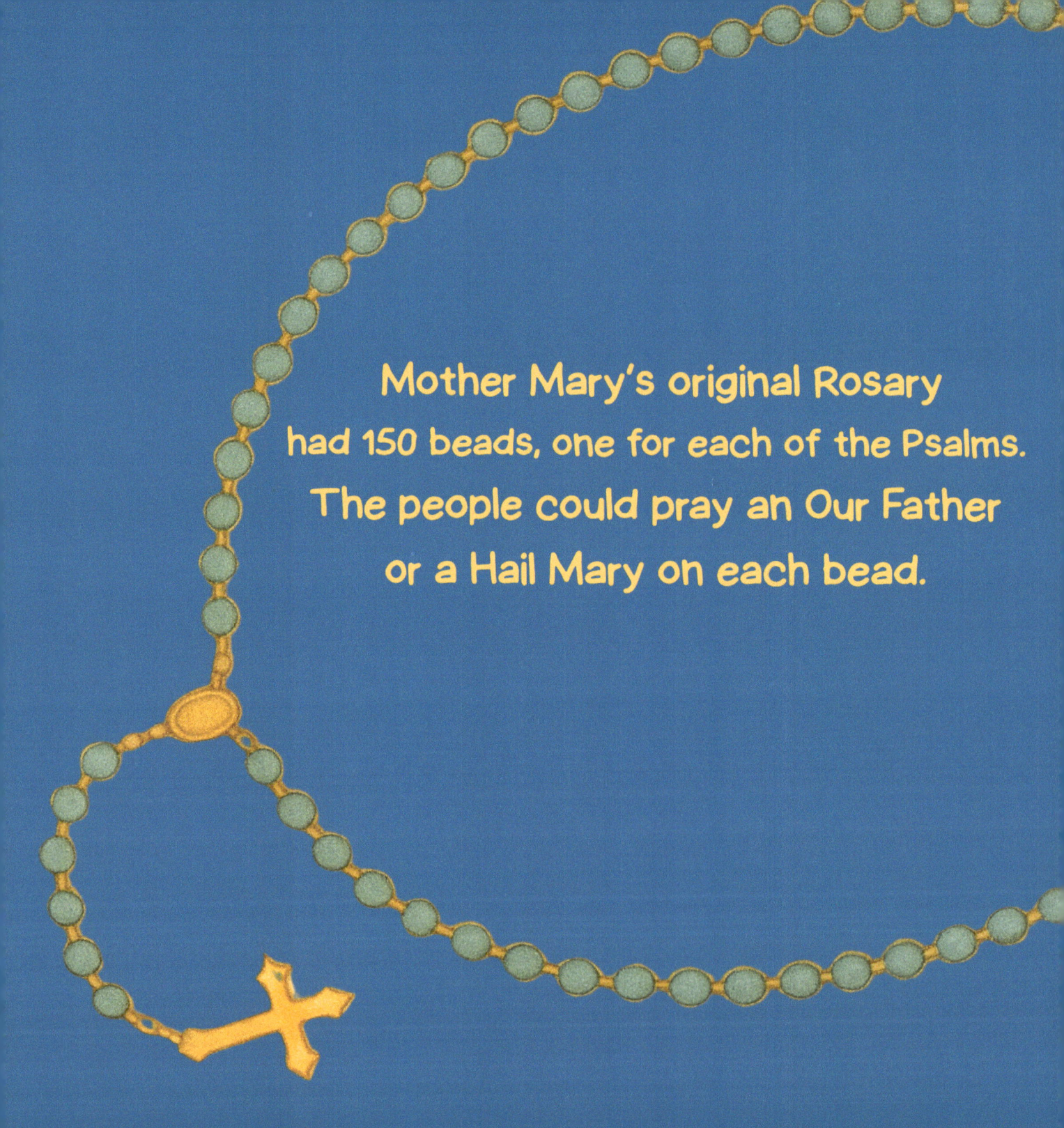

Mother Mary's original Rosary had 150 beads, one for each of the Psalms. The people could pray an Our Father or a Hail Mary on each bead.

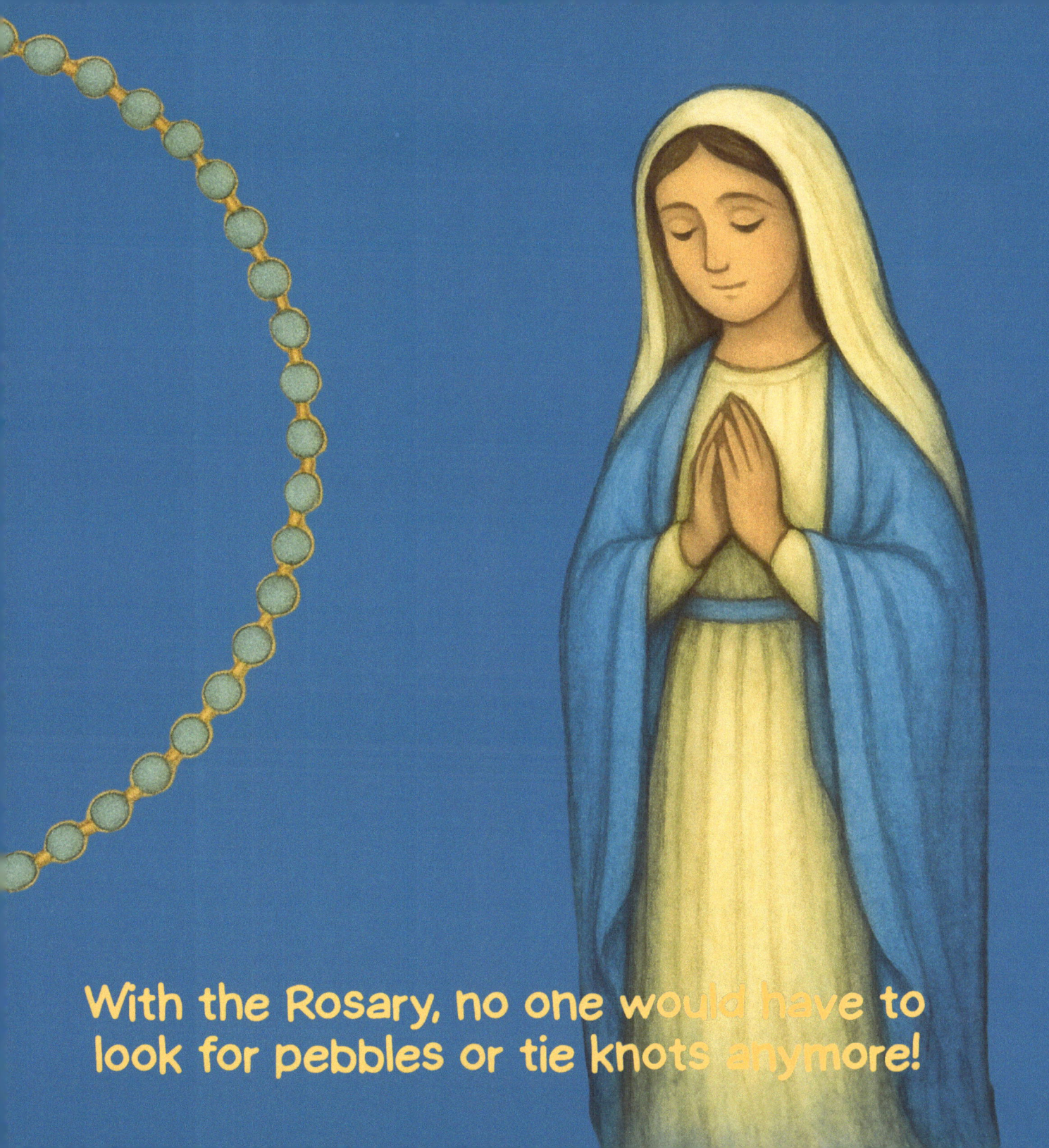

With the Rosary, no one would have to look for pebbles or tie knots anymore!

St. Dominic began to teach people everywhere how to pray the Rosary and think of Jesus.

People began saying the Rosary in their homes.
Over time, special prayers were added to the beginning of the Rosary. On the Crucifix, people said a prayer proclaiming what the Church believes. Then, on the new beads, they said an Our Father and three Hail Marys: One for Faith, One for Hope, and One for Love.

Using the rest of the beads, people started to meditate, to think really hard, about specific times in the lives of Jesus and Mary as they prayed.

Over time, the look of the Rosary changed. Eventually, the Rosary came to have 59 beads.

About 500 years ago, a different monk who was also named Dominic, Dominic of Prussia, divided the Rosary into 5 sections. Each section consisted of 1 Our Father and 10 Hail Marys. He also added the Glory Be prayer

Each section became known as a Decade of the Rosary, because the word decade means ten.

Pope Saint Pius V divided the Rosary into "Mysteries" – one Mystery for each decade. These Mysteries were not the kind of Mysteries people need to solve!

These were the Mysteries of the lives of Jesus and His Mother: Their lives were divided into the Joyful times, the Sorrowful times, and the Glorious times.

Later, Pope Saint John Paul II gave us five more Mysteries to shed more light on the life of Jesus. These were called the Luminous Mysteries.

People reflect on different Mysteries throughout the week

Monday and Saturday
Joyful Mysteries

Tuesday and Friday
Sorrowful Mysteries

Thursday
Luminous Mysteries

Sunday and Wednesday
Glorious Mysteries

JOYFUL

Annunciation

Presentation

Nativity of Jesus

Visitation

Finding Jesus in the Temple

MYSTERIES

LUMINOUS

Baptism in the Jordan

Transfiguration

Announcement of the

Wedding at Cana

Coming of the Kingdom

Institution of the Eucharist

MYSTERIES

SORROWFUL

Agony in the Garden

Carrying of the Cross

Crowning

MYSTERIES

Ascension

Crowning of Our Lady

MYSTERIES

A little over 100 years ago, Our Lady appeared with the Rosary to three Shepherd children in Fatima, Portugal.

She added one more prayer to the end of each decade, called The Fatima Prayer.

Today, people all over the World say the Rosary every day.

You can say the Rosary too!

Here is how to say the Rosary!!

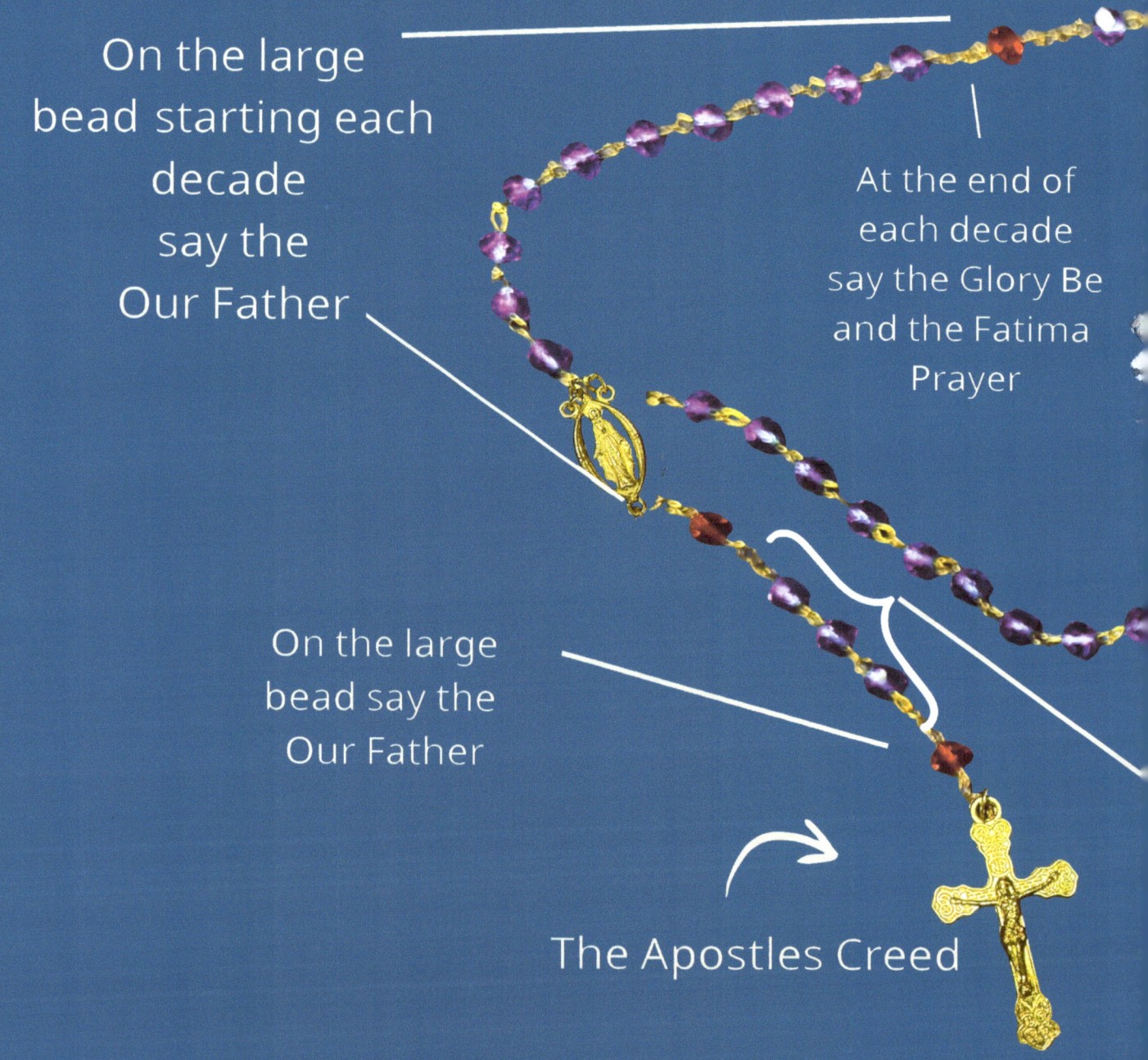

On the large bead starting each decade say the Our Father

At the end of each decade say the Glory Be and the Fatima Prayer

On the large bead say the Our Father

The Apostles Creed

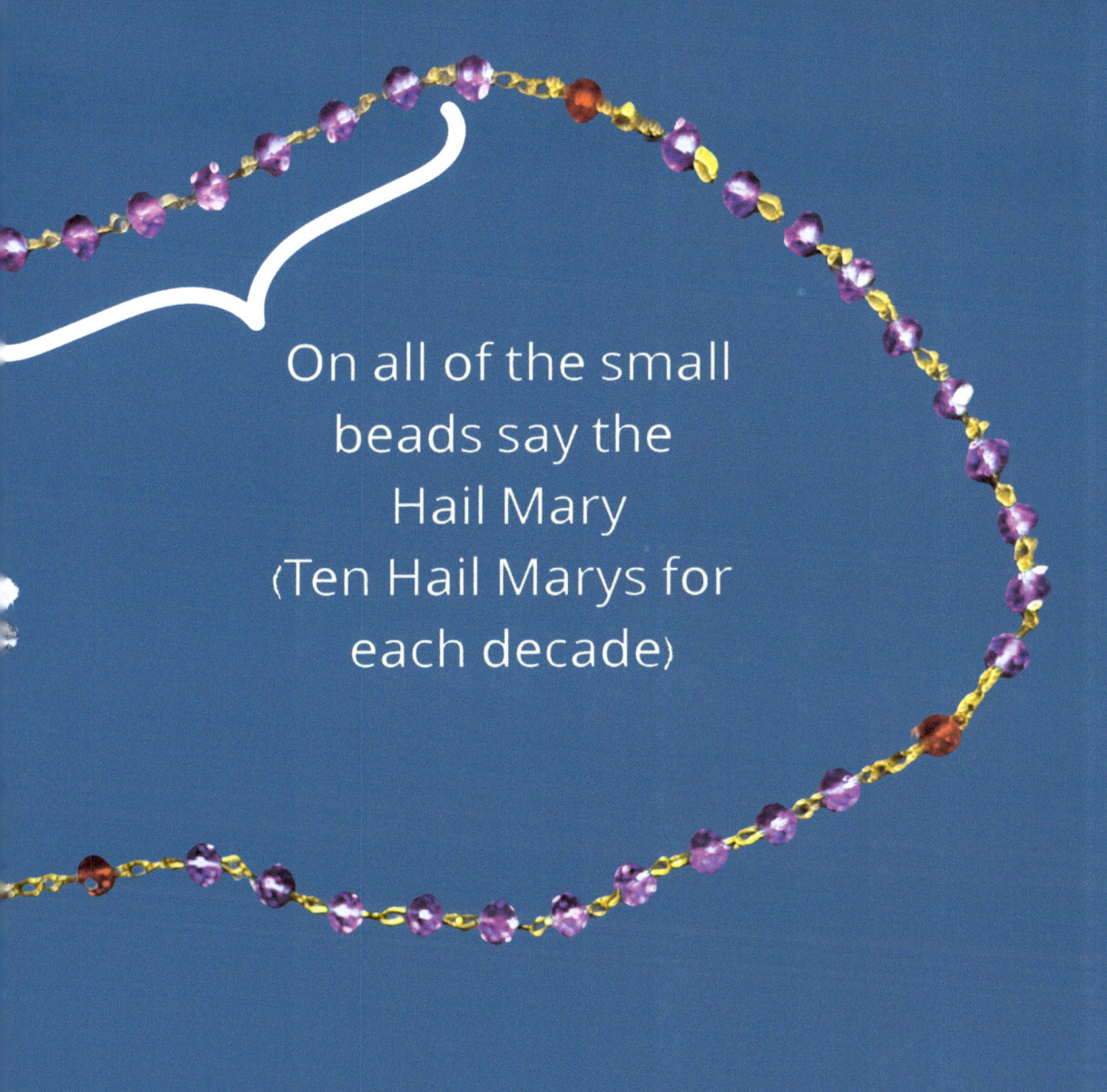

On all of the small beads say the Hail Mary (Ten Hail Marys for each decade)

On the three small beads say the Hail Mary, followed by the Glory Be

How to Make the Sign of the Cross

The Prayers of the Rosary

The Apostles' Creed

I believe in God,
the Father Almighty,
Creator of heaven and earth,
and in Jesus Christ, His only Son, our Lord,
who was conceived by the Holy Spirit,
born of the Virgin Mary,
suffered under Pontius Pilate,
was crucified, died and was buried;
He descended into hell;
on the third day He rose again from the dead;
He ascended into heaven,
and is seated at the right hand of God the Father Almighty;
from there He will come to judge the living and the dead.
I believe in the Holy Spirit,
the Holy Catholic Church,
the communion of Saints,
the forgiveness of sins,
the resurrection of the body,
and life everlasting.

Glory be

Glory Be to the Father and to the Son and to the Holy Spirit, as it was in the beginning is now, and ever shall be world without end.

Our Father

Our Father, who art in heaven,
Hallowed be Thy Name.
Thy Kingdom come.
Thy Will be done,
on earth as it is in Heaven.
Give us this day our daily bread.
And forgive us our trespasses,
as we forgive those who trespass against us.
And lead us not into temptation,
but deliver us from evil. Amen.

The Hail Mary

Hail Mary, full of grace, the Lord is with thee. Blessed art thou among women, and blessed is the fruit of thy womb, Jesus.
Holy Mary, Mother of God, pray for us sinners, now and at the hour of our death. Amen

The Fatima Prayer

O my Jesus, forgive us our sins, save us from the fires of hell, and lead all souls to heaven, especially those in most need of Your mercy